33 pieces

Rebecca Belmore

ESSAYS BY DOT TUER AND BARBARA FISCHER

PERFORMANCE CHRONOLOGY COMPILED BY JESSIE CARYL

BLACKWOOD GALLERY, UNIVERSITY OF TORONTO AT MISSISSAUGA

JANUARY 15 – FEBRUARY 18, 2001

33 pieces

CURATED BY BARBARA FISCHER

Blackwood Gallery, UTM

"33 pieces," installation view

Bury My Heart, 2000

Appearing Acts: Rebecca Belmore's 33 pieces

Rebecca Belmore has been making work as a performance artist for nearly fifteen years. But due to the nature of the medium – usually a singular event – only those who know the artist well can glean the depth and intensity of that work. When I asked her if she might be interested in developing an exhibition specifically centered on her performances (through objects and documents), it gradually became clear that this was not an appropriate avenue for her. Documentation of her performances in photography or video had always been incidental, if not altogether secondary. Where it existed, it had been initiated by others. The concerns of Belmore's work, I learned, lie elsewhere: in a particular place, with a particular audience and in relation to particular contextual, historical and "imagined" geographies.[1]

The proposed exhibition, therefore, evolved into an artist-in-residence project where the gallery served as temporary studio and became a socially active space for its entire duration. Named after the thirty-three pieces of the human spinal column, the exhibition situated past works as the invisible point of departure (the backbone) for a series of new works in diverse media. The new works represent aspects of Belmore's ongoing personal and political interests as an artist of Anishinabe descent, her concerns with actualities rather than abstractions.

Indian
Land

Throughout Belmore's work, common symbols are shaken up to take on different meanings. Against the flow of common understanding, they become troubled by what they do
not show, by the absences they construct and the ironies they assume. In Santa Fe in
1995 Belmore revealed the fetishism of tourism in *Tourist Act #1* when she choked herself on spicy tamales while reciting the names of dozens of galleries devoted to objects of
tribal art. She satirized Hollywood's nostalgia film *Pocahontas* in the title of her 1989 performance, *Patty Wagon Polka Haunt Us,* staged at the Thunder Bay Indian Friendship
Centre.

Above all, Belmore is a wordsmith with visual means, such as when she is *Rising to the
Occasion* for a visit of British Royals to Thunder Bay in 1987, together with eleven other
"angry crinolines," in an event conceptualized and organized by Lynne Sharman.[2] In
Belmore's costume for the event, braids of black hair stand up in the air and her dress is
cobbled together from tea cups and saucers, tourist treasures and beaver-dam twigs, at
once mimicry of Royalty and subversion of the colonized subject. She impersonates to
undo the stringent constraints of language and images. In *Five Sisters* stereotyped representations of Native women are eclipsed by their obvious staging. She impersonates to
gather power in the imaginary, intensely syncretic figure of *High Tech Teepee Trauma
Mama,* who reappears at different sites, on occasions of trauma and of need, to symbolize
strength drawn on all means at her disposal.

Belmore trips up meanings, creating havoc with its conventions and skilfully turning the
trickeries of language on themselves. Symbols betray their former purpose, such as when
the tools of Canadian nationalism and the constructs of national identity (symbols such as
the flag and national anthem) become signs of territorial subjugation and disputed land. In
1988 Belmore set herself up in a mock display case in front of the Thunder Bay Art
Gallery to support the Lubicon Cree's ongoing struggles over unresolved land claims –

just as the Olympic torch passed through the city and was celebrated with big fanfare at city hall.[3] Shell's sponsorship of an exhibition of First Nations' treasures, "The Spirit Sings," mounted at the Glenbow Museum in conjunction with the Olympics, became a lightning rod for the Lubicon protest; the Alberta government had sanctioned the oil company's drilling on Lubicon land. With a Shell logo pinned to her chest and a Canadian flag pinned to her back, Belmore made herself into an apparent museum *Artifact #671B* – her body the register of the fetishized myth of a bygone aboriginal culture and, as supported by Shell, the implicitly cynical forsaking of the present-day realities of First Nations' struggles.

In *Indian Land,* a work in this exhibition, the Canadian flag becomes a symbol of oppression – a signature on charted and contained territories. A mountainous landscape formed of innumerable paper souvenir flags mounted on the wall represents, in fact, the profile of an Indian (as found on the American nickel) tipped on its back. The area that is bounded by the flags is "Indian land." The flags' shadows flutter like ceremonial feathers (set into motion by a small fan) in this subtle subversion of Canadian possession.

Oka,
Ipperwash,
Burnt
Church ...

Even the simplest, sometimes least visible of means are used to make visual language churn and choke on its representations. In an untitled work in the exhibition, an application of white plaster on the white wall of the gallery bears in stencilled impressions place names that now stand for specific First Nations' struggles. *Oka,* the Mohawk Warriors' defence of sacred grounds against private interests; *Ipperwash,* the shooting of Dudley George in the protests over land rights; the dispute over lobster fishing rights at *Burnt Church;* and the founding of the new territory of *Nunavut.* The names stand for places and events as much as for deep lines of conflict, where official state policy and private interests infringed upon Native rights and claims; where the limits of language were tested in physical disputes; and where the stake of First Nations' struggles was thrown into sharp relief. As geography becomes history each event, in turn, indelibly marks the political landscape. Yet, in Belmore's work the names seem to appear only when viewed at an oblique angle, when the gallery light casts the shadows of the wall relief. A small tuft of black hair, affixed to the bottom of the list, recalls the tip of a brush whereby the relief poignantly suggests the writing of a First Nations history that is in the making (a history of events incised into locations), but it may also suggest a simultaneous disappearance of that history, as white on white may refer to the invisibility that always seems to threaten the presence of Native history in Canada.

In Belmore's understated work the nodal points of history intertwine with the subjects of her own performances, her interest in historical (dis)appearances. In *August 29, 1990,* a performance that embeds in its title the beginning of the Mohawk Nation's uprising at

Kanesatake and Kahnawake near Montreal, Belmore twists the effects of white history into a rope of knotted rags that she wraps around her neck. Attempting to sing the national anthem in the two official languages (French and English) she nearly chokes herself to signify her own (and others') loss of the language of her family, elders and Nation. However, in the context of the Oka crisis, she also presented an eloquent image for the choking of the voice of Native activism. As Alfred Young Man has argued, as Native peoples have resorted to self-defence in the face of guns, barricades and television manipulation, they have found themselves outnumbered, outgunned and yet, in the communications media, made to look like the aggressors rather than defenders of their lands.[4]

Saskatoon

… also appears in Belmore's subtle enumeration. Just over a year ago (in what has been revealed as common practice), police took two Native men to the Queen Elizabeth II Power Plant on the edges of the city in the midst of winter and left them there to die. In one of her most complex performances, staged at AKA Gallery in Saskatoon and part of her recurrent appearance as *High Tech Teepee Trauma Mama,* Belmore presented several distinct episodes, each centered on searing images bearing reference to that nightmarish event. At one point she dances in cowboy hat and gear to country music, apparently intoxicated and having a good time, while cop-car revolving lights provide for an unsettling disco atmosphere, rife with tension. In another sequence of events an industrial fan is used to blow blood dripping from a feather up against a wall; if the process is reminiscent of Jackson Pollock's work and possibly refers to its reputed source in First Nations sand drawings, it emerges here written in blood. But the performance begins with a more harrowing image: an intense production line where Belmore and a partner work at a frenzied pace dipping jackets in plaster and hanging them on hooks in the gallery to dry and stiffen. The grey plaster turns white just as the men's bodies turned to ice at the QEII Power Plant. In this *Indian Factory* I find it difficult not to see the outlines of northern genocide.

In the current exhibition the events of that winter return as a haunting echo – not only by way of the name of Saskatoon. Following the fault-lines of historical and present-day trauma, patches of plaster-stiffened rags are mounted in one of the upper corners of the room, like small ghosts on their way out of the gallery space; a large, white paper shirt suggests the hollow absence of a body and an as-yet unwritten text;[5] pencil shavings and graphite have left a black trace along the wall on their way to the pile on the floor, in what is a visual mark of labour without words; and a shredded manuscript has been made into the white shape of a curled-up body (the manuscript was produced by Belmore in a day-long performance titled *Manifesto,* staged in Toronto in 1999). While each element is distinct, all work together to make erasure, absence and silence visible, and cast their shadows in a space that becomes ever-more haunted.

The space of the gallery is, in this way, an integral object (subject?) of Belmore's work. The installation makes it into a charged symbolic space where even the blank of the wall is twisted into meaning, as much as are the floor and the ceiling. The horizon line of the American-nickel Indian's profile implicates and claims the floor beneath us, and so does the title *Indian Land* implicate the ground on which we stand. White walls now bear the cultural connotations of the word "white," and these meanings are punctuated by hardened plaster that refers to ghosts and to ice, by shredded texts on white paper, and by the shadows of history everywhere in the "white cube" – the space of the gallery that was designed to absent history. The connotations of this space are sharply focused in the grey-blue glass eyes that Belmore has embedded in the wall at the entrance. They subject the viewer to the colour of the institutional gatekeepers' eyes and their implied surveillance (in both of which I feel myself uneasily implicated).

... Nunavut (Inuktitut for "our land")

Certain elements recur again and again in ways that do not necessarily imply repeated meanings, the same univocal signification. At each turn there are inflections and different takes, some specific in their reference and others more broadly symbolic. Take the element of the tree. Inasmuch as it is a Canadian archetype (the "lone pine" in the paintings of the Group of Seven; the motif of the Maple Leaf, etc.), its "loneliness" now registers the extent of our greed and environmental destruction. Belmore has pulled both meanings, apparently opposites, into ironic proximity in a wall work where two denuded spruce trunks (they had served their term as Christmas trees) cut into small pieces are mounted back together, but bottom to bottom, as if in a reflection of each other: uprooted and dismembered. Symbolically speaking, the work suggests the destruction of the lone pine and thereby a destruction of the myth of untamed wilderness. Its meanings are doubled further, however, in that the pieces of the tree look like the vertebrae of a spine that's been re-assembled on the wall by emphatically large construction nails.

It seems that it is in this sense that the tree is an especially significant element or preoccupation in Belmore's work. *Black Cloud,* a charred and twisted piece of wood, is suspended above a bed of salt – as white as the base of the Canadian flag or as January in this snowy northern land. The dark cloud may be read as an ominous sign over Canadian territories. Spiked with nails, the charred wood may be staked but it is also an ambiguous new tool. Showing evidence of persistent and intensive labour, it is as much a sculpture

Ayumee-aawach Oomama-mowan: Speaking to Their Mother, 1991

as a representation of history and the suggestion of a weapon. It represents symbolically what sculpture can be or what still needs to be done: intense repetition, exhausting exertion and inestimable duration.

In the performance *For Nunavut,* staged on the occasion of the official inception of the new territory of Nunavut on April 1st, 1999, Belmore read the statistics for the new territory as reported in rather sceptical assessments in the papers that day – 772,260 square miles; almost entirely above the tree line; landscape dominated by tundra, rock, snow and ice; the largest Native land-claim settlement in Canadian history; population 27,100 of which 85% are Inuit; facing problems including high unemployment, substance abuse and suicide rates.... If the reports suggested paternalistic doubt (can the Inuit do it?), Belmore's actions countered the message using its own means. Surrounded by trouble lights she pounded nails as high as she could reach into a large log that stood upright in a mound of snow in the centre of a room at the art school. Her pounding counted for rather than against hope. Packing snow onto the log, her gesture (rather than representing a sealed and troubled fate) was to make the log a sculptural monument that represented both task and accomplishment. The monumental scale and scope of this work are also found in another work – a large, exquisitely crafted wooden megaphone that Belmore built during a residency in Banff in 1991 – through which an ever-growing community has found a voice, participating in collective action. Known as *Ayumee-aawach Oomama-mowan: Speaking to Their Mother,* the megaphone is at once sculpture and tool, and has since been used by Native leaders and community activists across the country as a means to speak to the earth and to address the earth as the mother of everything, in language that needs no translation.

Rose

If her "mother-tongue" appears in the bifurcated titles of the majority of her performances and installations – *Mushkegokwe/Swampwoman* (1989), *Ihkwewak Ka-ayamihwat: Means Women Who Are Speaking* (1989) and *Kiskino-tuma-kaawin-ninee: One Who Is Leading* (1992), among others – Belmore has often talked about and included in her work references to the loss of her native language and the repercussions of that loss across the generations of her family. While her grandmother spoke Ojibway she did not speak English; Belmore herself grew up speaking English but did not learn Ojibway. It is her mother who represents the turning point in that history as she wanted her daughter to learn the new way of life. In this exhibition Belmore remembers her mother, though in a work that is more than personal recollection as it turns on turning points. A shelf with tea service – a teapot and kettle, cups and tea bags, sugar and lemons – also includes a tray that bears Queen Elizabeth II's portrait. A symbol for the British crown to which Canada remains colonial subject, and which it honours in such monumental sites as the Saskatoon Power Plant, the portrait on the tray now becomes servant implicitly. The work symbolically reverses colonial history, including that of her mother, who supported her family by mending clothes, cleaning house and doing odd jobs for Anglo Canadians. Belmore has made this reversal explicit by placing a lit candle in an English teacup as ritual offering to her late mother's portrait. It is to this commemorative image also that a fresh rose is offered, first by the artist and then, appropriately, by the gallery attendants.

But it is not just reversal that Belmore has in mind. She has set up a kitchen table with chairs – between her mother's portrait and the tea-service shelf – which becomes, for the duration of the exhibition, a place to meet and talk and listen over tea. It is a hospitable place, an open invitation for whatever may take place in a location that over the centuries has excluded immediate exchange between people(s) in its insistence on silence and contemplation. Recorded voices underline the actual conversations that may take place at this table; they are presented like gifts, hidden in closed and half-open cardboard boxes. Amongst them is an interview with James Luna, a friend and Native American performance artist from California to whom Belmore also pays tribute in this exhibition.

Manifesto, 2001 (detail)

Manifesto (performance), 1999

Manifesto, 2001 (detail)

Mounted way up in a circle of lights, shiny yellow shoes stand for the artist whose name implies the light that radiates from the moon. I have rarely found the effect of lights as hopeful and beautiful as they are in this place, amongst the histories and thoughts that interlock in Rebecca Belmore's installation.

Barbara Fischer

Notes

1. Marilyn Burgess, "The Imagined Geographies of Rebecca Belmore," *Parachute* 93 (Jan./Feb./March 1999), pp. 12–20. This essay is the most thorough discussion of Belmore's work to date.

2. Charlotte Townsend-Gault has discussed this work in detail in her essay on Rebecca Belmore in *Land Spirit Power* (Ottawa: National Gallery of Canada, 1991), p. 117.

3. Rebecca Belmore noted with pride that the local paper reporting the events of that day reproduced a larger picture of the performance event at the gallery than of the official events honouring the Olympic torch at city hall.

4. Alfred Young Man, "The Savage Civilian and the work of Rebecca Belmore," in Daina Augaitis and Sylvie Gilbert, eds. *Between Views* (Banff, Alberta: Walter Phillips Gallery, 1991), pp. 37–39.

5. A poem by Kateri Damm is pinned inside the shirt and takes the place of an apparent absent text on the paper of the shirt.

> Eyes lowered body bent forward
> move slowly with care
> through this wilderness that is my love
> then when you leave there will only be echoes of
> your sounds
> a barely discernible path
> and a few ashes from your fire
> swirling in the wind
> like a warning
> then the wilderness will remain
> untamed as it should be
> and you will emerge with clean hands
> and the will to survive

Indian Land, 2001

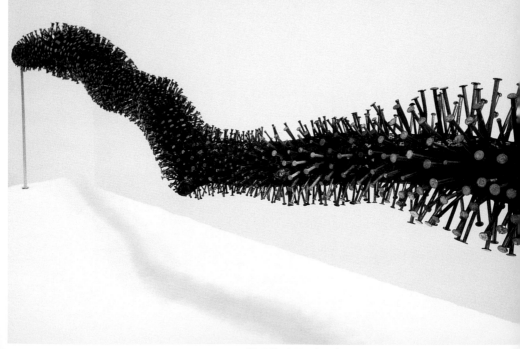

Black Cloud, 2001 (detail)

Untitled, 2001 (detail)

Creation or Death; We Will Win, 1991

Performing Memory

The art of storytelling in the work of Rebecca Belmore

Mister Luna, 2001

Rebecca Belmore is a sculptor and performer, a creator of installations and actions. She is an Anishinabe artist, an interpreter of history. Above all she is a storyteller. In the early 1990s there was a moment when, as a storyteller, Belmore felt she was being asked to tell all: to spill forth words that tore open the wounds of colonial oppression and racism. In being asked to tell all she wondered if she was telling too much, and decided to gather stories around her through gestures and objects rather than through words. In her performances her body became a cipher for the way in which the scars of history are embodied; in her installations her objects became offerings to a landscape that harbours the residue of ancestral memory. Through her gestures and objects Belmore has produced over the last ten years a powerful testimony to art as a process of concretizing acts of remembering and resistance, dreaming and mourning. After the exhibition closes or the performance ends, the material traces of her artistic process live on through their continual retelling. What follows here is my retelling of an exhibition held at the Blackwood Gallery in Mississauga in February 2001, and of the insights Belmore has shared with me about her artmaking.

On a bitter cold winter day, with brilliant sunshine a fool's gold in a harsh north wind, I drive out to the Blackwood Gallery to meet Rebecca Belmore. Her exhibition, a performative work in progress, is almost complete. Belmore has spent a month as an artist in residence, creating a series of individual works that will form the component whole at the closing of the show rather than at its beginning. When I arrive on the grounds of Erindale College where the gallery is located, Belmore has just returned from lighting a fire and charring a log, ducking behind trees when the security car drives around. The log, which she will subsequently pound with nails and suspend above a bed of salt, is resonant with stories that reach back from the visceral moment of the work's creation to the ephemeral recesses of the artist's memory. Embedded in this work in progress are many allusions: to drums beating in the pounding of nails; to salt as an instrument of colonial trade and a simile for snow; to trees as natural monuments in a culture of spiritual clear-cutting; to shorn limbs as metaphors for our bodily existence. Like all the pieces in the exhibition the log is alive with stories woven into its making, stories that fill the gallery with murmurs of poetry and affirmation, past injustices and present struggles for self-determination.

During our meeting we sit at a country kitchen table in one corner of the exhibition space, where tea can be sipped and recorded tapes of several of Belmore's performances watched. On the wall behind us Belmore has placed a single rose and a picture of her mother standing in front of a log cabin; on a small shelf on an adjacent wall, a teacup service sits on a tray bearing the Queen's portrait. Beside us, subtly embedded in drywall, a pair of glass eyes watches us. The picture of the artist's mother and the tea service form a collective memorial to the meeting of indigenous and imperial histories. The glass eyes are uncanny reminders that objects can see you as well as you see them, that land-scape is not inert but acts upon one. Belmore tells me that her mother, whose name was Rose, used to stay alone in the trapper's cabin shown in the picture. Isolated deep in the Ontario woods, Rose kept company with a transistor radio. One day, as night descended, the batteries in the radio began to die, and the crackling noises of other people's words slowly faded away into an eerie silence. Belmore tells me that when she was a child her mother took her by canoe to the island where she was born. Years later, after her mother died, she decided to canoe back to the island, but although she recognized the shoreline and the landmarks she couldn't find it. Silence, Belmore seems to be telling me, can be more powerful than words; the land harbours memories that we cannot always locate.

In 1991, Belmore travelled to Cuba to perform during the Havana Biennial. She chose as her site a historic colonial building, Castillo de la Fuerza (Castle of Strength), in which a staircase wound up the sides of an internal courtyard. Using a long red rope to tie her ankles and wrists together and gag her mouth, she struggled up the staircase, scooping up and sweeping away sand that lay across each worn step. The viewers gathered in the courtyard and at the top of the stairs could hear her exertion and panting, see the strain of her movements. Occasionally, she let a scream escape from her mouth. In this primal action, stripped of words and props, she conjured the ghosts of slavery, the silenced looks of oppression, the sweat of Cuba's sugar fields. In 2000, Belmore travelled to Montana to perform Bury My Heart, a work whose title honours the dead of Wounded Knee. A violinist played at the perimeter of a plot of land transformed into a field of mud by a water sprinkler, while Belmore dug in the wet earth with her bare hands to uncover a hole filled with blood. In the hole she placed a pioneer chair that she was staining, as well as a bouquet of carnations, which she then pulled out, bloodied and bedraggled. As her feet sunk into the oozing earth, her hands awash in blood and her white dress splattered with mud, her body and the remembering of history became intertwined. Through sparse and silent gestures Belmore had excavated the spirits of the dead.

In Canada, the dominant culture of English colonialism has denuded the landscape of its sacred elements, repressed the spirits of the dead. The Group of Seven's paintings, as symbols of a nationalist heritage, empty the northern woods of human traces. Nature and culture, land and body, indigenous and imperial histories are not conjoined but severed, a severing that finds its discursive echoes in the narratives of thinkers who have shaped our social imagination. Northrop Frye, an esteemed literary critic who searched for an answer to the question "where is here," constructed an embattled vision of Canadian civilization as a bulwark against a hostile wilderness. Frye's writing on the Canadian landscape was doubly negative: negative for the overwhelming emptiness of an untamed nature and for the way in which technology has obliterated the landscape. For Frye, "Canada is a country in which nature makes a direct impression on the artist's mind, an impression of its primeval lawlessness and moral nihilism, its indifference to the supreme value placed on life within human society. Its faceless, mindless unconsciousness fosters life without benevolence and destroys it without malice."[1]

In Frye's fixation on nature as a cultural void, the Canadian landscape (whether the craggy rocks and lonely pines portrayed by the Group of Seven or the inhospitable regions of the imagination mapped by Margaret Atwood in her book on Canadian literature, *Survival)* serves as the backdrop for Canada's historical narrative of an orderly progression from settler colony to modern nation. Memories of conquest and resistance are vanquished from a representational field, their absence papered over by mythologies of pristine wilderness or technological progress. Yet, although they are excised and disavowed, these memories still linger, still trouble, still disturb, whether in the collective uprising of the Mohawk Nation to protect their burial grounds at Oka, or in a quiet moment walking in the northern bush when suddenly the trees begin to whisper and stare. The condition of historical amnesia in which landscape has been depeopled is a traumatic one. It is this condition, this trauma, that Belmore addresses in her performances and installations.

As we sit talking in the gallery this winter afternoon, Belmore tells me that she has transformed the gallery into a landscape, one in which the objects speak to memories of historical conflict. Across the room from where we sit a pile of wood shavings forms beneath a pencil sharpener; near it lies a shredded paper figure curled up into a fetal position on the floor. In the corner hang rags dipped in plaster and beside them a white stiffened shirt. Between the rags and shirt, stencilled into a patch of white plaster relief, are the names of confrontations between First Nations and government authorities: Oka, Burnt Church, Ipperwash and Saskatoon. On the far wall tiny souvenir Canadian flags are arranged to resemble the profile of the American Indian from the United States nickel. Fluttering in a fan-propelled wind, the diminutive flags shed their nationalist identity. They look more like dancing feathers, their shadows like clouds passing overhead, their profile like a mountain. Together, these pieces form the backbone of Belmore's narrative, retelling stories that we may have heard before in another guise through the mass media or through history books. Each piece also references a material element used by Belmore in a previous performance, linking questions of who tells stories to a conjoining of land and body, indigenous memory and imperial conquest.

In her use of pencil and paper Belmore takes European instruments for recording history and transforms them. Through the stories that are told about her objects the past is preserved as oral culture. The pencil sharpener and shredded paper figure are the material traces of a performance work by Belmore, in which she sat in a storefront window and wrote by hand in pencil from sunrise to sunset. As she wrote she spoke the words, which viewers heard broadcast through loudspeakers on the street. During the performance time was marked by the movement of the sun and the repetitive action of sharpening the pencil as it wore down. The significance of the manuscript Belmore produced through this day-long action was not in its written form, but in the labour embodied in the reams of paper and in the disembodiment of language that viewers witnessed as they watched her silent, glassed-in body mouth the words. By tearing up the manuscript and shaping from its remnants a bodily presence in the gallery, Belmore creates a memorial to the lived experiences that the written documents of history excise or misrepresent. The shredded paper figure also has an immediate historical resonance to the stiff white shirt that hangs on the wall. Both these objects render visible the legacies of a racist history, alluding to the frozen bodies of First Nation's men in Saskatoon, who in the dead of winter in 2000 were taken by police to the outskirts of the city and abandoned to die in the snow, without shoes or coats. The plaster rags, in turn, are echoes of the stiffened white shirt, embodying the repetitive actions of washing, scrubbing and cleaning away negative stereotypes. As part of a landscape in which the spirits of the dead are remembered and mourned, the rags become the guardians of memory: clouds, dreams and ghosts.

In 1991, as the mass-media coverage of the 1990 Oka confrontation began to solidify into a historical narrative that silenced First Nations voices and their stories of the uprising, Belmore created an enormous megaphone that she used in a series of performance actions titled *Ayumee-aawach Oomama-mowan: Speaking to Their Mother.* The megaphone served as a flash point of protest and storytelling in different locations across Canada, from Banff National Park, to the Prime Minister's Sussex Drive residence, to a northern Saskatchewan logging blockade. On each occasion Belmore would approach the megaphone and speak first, addressing her words to the earth. Then, others who were gathered around would take their turn. As they spoke into the megaphone an echo could be heard. With the earth returning words scattered in the wind back to the speaker, stories were now embedded in the landscape. Ten years later, as we sit and talk within another kind of landscape, one filled with the material traces of Belmore's performative actions, she tells me that she does not have beginnings in her work but only endings. Yet, through her artistic process of fusing body and earth, her endings are always the beginnings of other stories, her stories are gifts of memory, her memory becomes a repository of history.

Dot Tuer

Note

1. Northrop Fyre, "The Narrative Tradition in English Language Poetry" in *The Bush Garden: Essays on the Canadian Imagination* (Toronto: Anansi, 1971), p. 146.

Rose (Part 2), 2001

Untitled, 2001

Rebecca Belmore Performance Chronology
compiled by Jessie Caryl

1987
Mukwa, for the opening of "Manitoulin Island: The Third Layer," Thunder Bay Art Gallery, Thunder Bay, Ontario

Rising to the Occasion, "Twelve Angry Crinolines," parade and video performance organized by Lynne Sharman, Thunder Bay, Ontario

I'm a High Tech Teepee Trauma Mama, Definitely Superior Art Gallery, Thunder Bay, Ontario

1988
Artifact #671B, protest in support of the Lubicon Cree, Thunder Bay Art Gallery, Thunder Bay, Ontario

I'm a High Tech Teepee Trauma Mama, for "Indian Days," Native Student Association Winter Carnival, Lakehead University, Thunder Bay, Ontario

HOWUH!, community-based performance project (with Allen Deleary), Definitely Superior Art Gallery/Thunder Bay Indian Friendship Centre, Thunder Bay, Ontario

This is a performance / This is not a performance, for "Souvenir from the Northern Front," Mayworks Festival, Toronto

1989
Crazy Old Woman Child, Indian Friendship Centre, Thunder Bay, Ontario

Patty Wagon Polka Haunt Us, Thunder Bay Indian Friendship Centre, Thunder Bay, Ontario

Ihkwewak Ka-ayamihwat II: Means Women Who Are Speaking, "Changers: A Spiritual Renaissance," National Arts and Crafts Corporation, Ottawa, Ontario (national touring exhibition); Harbourfront, Toronto 1989; Owens Art Gallery, Mount Allison University, Sackville, 1991; Tom Thomson Memorial Gallery, Owen Sound, 1991

1990
Trauma Mama, "Duster Cabaret," Western Front, Vancouver, British Columbia

A Painting, A Talk, A Ritual, Agnes Etherington Art Centre, Kingston, Ontario

August 29, 1990, Première biennale d'art actuel de Québec, Quebec City, Quebec

1991
Ayumee-aawach Oomama-mowan: Speaking to Their Mother "Between Views", Walter Phillips Gallery, Banff Centre for the Arts, Banff, Alberta (national tour, 1991–92)

August 29, 1990, Walter Phillips Gallery, Banff Centre for the Arts, Banff, Alberta

Creation or Death: We Will Win, IV Bienal de la Habana, Havana, Cuba

1993
Road Trip West: 7 Concession Stands, for "Indian Princesses and Cowgirls: Stereotypes from the Frontier," Galerie Oboro, Montreal, Quebec

Untitled, Student graduation banquet, Sioux Lookout, Ontario

Are We Violent?, Sioux Lookout Anti-Racism Committee, Sioux Lookout, Ontario

1994
affiliation/affliction (with Reona Brass), Recontre internationale d'art performance de Quebec, Le Lieu, Quebec

1995
Tourist Act #1, Institute of American Indian Arts, Santa Fe, New Mexico

From the Same Earth, "Longing and Belonging: From the Faraway Nearby," SITE Santa Fe, New Mexico

1996
Ayumee-aawach Oomama-mowan: Speaking to Their Mother, borrowed by the Assembly of First Nations on First Nations Day in protest of First Ministers conference, Ottawa, Ontario

1997
For Dudley, 7a * 11d Performance Festival, Toronto, Ontario

Five Sisters, for "Indian Princesses and Cowgirls: Stereotypes from the Frontier" (national touring exhibition circulated by Presentation House Gallery), Presentation House Gallery, Vancouver, BC, 1997; Dunlop Art Gallery, Regina, Saskatchewan, 1999

1998
Canadian Performance Art Tour, various cities, Germany

1999
Manifesto, "Time Time Time," FADO, Zsa Zsa Gallery, Toronto, Ontario

Don't take your guns to town, University of New Brunswick Art Centre, Fredericton, New Brunswick

For Nunavut, White Mountain Academy of Art, Elliott Lake, Ontario

2000
Bury My Heart, "Material Culture," Paris Gibson Square Museum, Great Falls, Montana

Rebecca Belmore

Solo Exhibitions

2001
33 pieces, Blackwood Gallery, Mississauga, Ontario

2000
on this ground, Rhode Island School of Design Museum of Art, Providence, Rhode Island

1999
Many/One, Galerie Optica, Montreal, Quebec

Dreamers, Keyano College Art Gallery, Fort McMurray, Alberta

1998
Untitled, Sacred Circle Gallery, Seattle, Washington

1993
Wana-na-wang-ong, Contemporary Art Gallery, Vancouver, British Columbia

Nah-doe-tah-moe-win: Means an Object That You Listen To (performance/installation), Gallery Saw, Ottawa, Ontario

Nah-doe-tah-moe-win: Means an Object That You Listen To, Niagara Artists' Centre, Saint Catherines, Ontario

Group Exhibitions

2000
"I. Witness," Edmonton Art Gallery, Edmonton, Alberta *(Many/One; in memory)*

"High Tech Storytellers," Interdisciplinary Arts Festival, TRIBE/AKA, Saskatoon, Saskatchewan *(The Indian Factory)*

"Material Culture," Paris Gibson Square Museum, Great Falls, Montana *(Many/One)*

1998
Sydney Biennial, Sydney, Australia *(Paradise)*

1997
"The Red River Crossing," Swiss Art Institute, New York, NY *(Us. With a Landscape.)*

"InSITE 97," San Diego, California *(Awasinake: On the Other Side)*

1996
"Liaisons," The Power Plant, Toronto, Ontario *(Temple)*

"Métissages," Galerie Optica, Montreal, Quebec *(Imposition* with Florence Belmore)

1995
"Longing and Belonging: From the Faraway Nearby," SITE Santa Fe, New Mexico *(New Wilderness)*

1994
"6th Native American Fine Arts Invitational," The Heard Museum, Phoenix, Arizona *(a blanket for "sarah")*

"Faret Tachikawa Art Project," Art Front Gallery, Tokyo, Japan *(I wait for the sun)*

"History 101: The Re-Search for Family," Forum for Contemporary Art, St. Louis, Missouri *(X mark)*

1993
"Stand," Erie Art Museum, Erie, Pennsylvania *(Shifting the North Line: 16 Pictures)*

"marginsofmemory," Art Gallery of Windsor, Windsor, Ontario *(Rising to the Occasion)*

"Stand, " Erie Art Museum, Erie, Pennsylvania *(Shifting the North Line: 16 Pictures)*

1992
"Land Spirit Power," National Gallery of Canada, Ottawa, Ontario *(Mawu-che-hitoowin: A Gathering of People for Any Purpose)*

1991
"okanata," A Space, Toronto, Ontario *(August 29, 1990)*

"Between Views," Walter Phillips Gallery, Banff, Alberta *(Ayumee-aawach-Oomama-mowan: Speaking to Their Mother)*

"Interrogating Identity," Grey Art Gallery, New York University *(Rising to the Occasion; True Grit)*

"A Likeness," Agnes Etherington Art Centre, Kingston, Ontario *(An Introspective)*

1990
"Multi-Media Works: A Native Perspective," AKA Gallery, Saskatoon, Saskatchewan *(Nah-doe-tah-moe-win: Means an Object That You Listen To)*

"Telling Things," Art Metropole, Toronto, Ontario *(Nah-doe-tah-moe-win: Means an Object That You Listen To)*

"Young Contemporaries 90," London Regional Art Gallery, London, Ontario *(Nah-doe-tah-moe-win: Means an Object That You Listen To; Ihkwewak Ka-ayamihwat: Means Women Who Are Speaking)*

1989
"Changers: A Spiritual Renaissance," National Arts and Crafts Corporation, Ottawa, Ontario *(Skirt Series)*

1986
"See Jane Sew Strontium," Definitely Superior Art Gallery, Thunder Bay, Ontario *(True Grit)*

"The New Traditionalists," Definitely Superior Art Gallery, Thunder Bay, Ontario *(Skirt Series)*

Selected Articles and Reviews

Barkhouse, Mary Anne, "Land, Spirit, Power," *Matriart: A Canadian Feminist Art Journal* 3:2 (1992), pp. 16–21.

Belmore, Rebecca, "Autonomous Aboriginal High-Tech Teepee Trauma Mama," *Canadian Theatre Review* 58 (Fall 1991).

wana-na-wang-ong: Rebecca Belmore, poetry by Florene Belmore; essay by Lee-Ann Martin (Vancouver, BC: Contemporary Art Gallery), 1993.

Burgess, Marilyn, "The Imagined Geographies of Rebecca Belmore," *Parachute* 93 (Jan./Feb./March 1999), pp. 12–20.

Chapman, Steve, Susan Jeffrey and Ruth Denny, "Art of the People," *Art Paper* 12:3 (Nov. 1992), pp. 9–11.

Dompierre, Louise and Fred Gaysek, "Liaisons: Rebecca Belmore, Wyn Geleynse, Roberto Pellegrinuzzi, Laurel Woodcock" (Toronto, Ontario: The Power Plant, 1996).

Durand, Guy Sioui, "Creative currents: Métissage merges Native and non-Native creativity," *Aboriginal Voices* 1:4 (Fall 1994), pp. 42–45.

"Exhibition explores spectacles of place: Appropriately enough, Santa Fe, a place as much imagined as real, is the site of an exhibit of works on our collective ideas about belonging (Longing and Belonging)," *Globe & Mail,* 4 Oct. 1995, pp. C1–2.

Fleming, Kathleen, "Longing and Belonging: From the Faraway Nearby," *Parachute* 82 (Apr./May/June 1996).

Fraser, Marie, Guy Sioui Durand, et al, "Métissages" (Saint-Jean-de-Jolie, Quebec: Centre du Sculpture, 1996).

Kelley, Caffyn, "Broken silence, visible wounds: Canadian artists expose social space with contradictions intact," *High Performance* 18:1–2 (Spring/Summer 1995).

Lacey, Liam, "Native artist puts new spin on the western," *Globe and Mail,* 22 Sept. 1990.

Laurence, Robin, "Rebecca Belmore: Wana-na-wang-ong," *Canadian Art* (Spring 1994).

Baert, Renee, "Marginsofmemory: Rebecca Belmore, Marlene Creates, Sarindar Dhaliwal, Wyn Geleynse, Jan Peacock, Jin-me Yoon, Sharyn Yuen" (Windsor, Ontario: Art Gallery of Windsor, 1994).

Martel, Richard, "Recontre internationale d'art performance de Québec," *INTER(Canada)* 62 (Summer 1995), p. i-xxviiip.

Miller, Edith, "Rebecca Belmore: Ihkwewak Ka-ayamihwat II: Means Women Who Are Speaking," *ARTSatlantic* 10:4 (Spring/Summer 1991), p. 52.

Mitchell, Charles Dee, "Introducing SITE Santa Fe," *Art in America* 83:10 (Oct. 1995), pp. 44–47.

Nemiroff, Diana, Robert Houle and Charlotte Townsend-Gault, "Land, Spirit, Power: First Nations at the National Gallery of Canada" (Ottawa, Ontario: National Gallery of Canada, 1992).

Phillips, Ruth, "Woodlands Indian Souvenir Art as Visual Text: Reinventing Iconology in the Post-Colonial Age," *Texts* 8 (Summer 1992).

Podedworny, Carol, "Okanata," *C* 32 (Fall 1991). "Realities of Ojibway culture pervasive in artist's work," *Halifax Chronicle Herald,* 30 Jan. 1991, p. C3.

Riddle, Mason, "Rebecca Belmore," *High Performance* 15 (Winter 1992), pp. 24–25.

Rushing, W. Jackson, "Contingent Histories, Aesthetic Politics," *New Art Examiner* (March 1993).

Seaton, Beth, "Indian Princesses and Cowgirls: Stereotypes from the Frontier – Rebecca Belmore," *Parachute* 69 (1993).

Sharman, L., "Making Art in the State of Texas," *Fuse* 15.

Tourbin, Dennis, "Visual Cadence," *Artscraft* 1:4.

Townsend-Gault, Charlotte, "Having Voices and Using Them," *Arts Magazine* (Feb. 1991), pp. 65–70.

Townsend-Gault, Charlotte, "Ritualizing ritual's rituals (ritual as a vehicle for personal and social negotiation in contemporary Native American Art)," *Art Journal* 51 (Fall 1992), pp. 51–58.

Townsend-Gault, Charlotte, "Rebecca Belmore," *Parachute* 74 (April / May / June 1994).

Tuer, Dot, "At the gates," *Canadian Art* (Spring 1998), pp. 72–78.

Valaskakis, Gail Guthrie and Marilyn Burgess, *Princesses indiennes et cowgirls: stereotypes de la frontiere / Indian Princesses and Cowgirls: Stereotypes from the Frontier,* bookwork by Rebecca Belmore (Montreal, Quebec: Oboro, 1995).

"Wana na wang ong," *Vancouver Sun,* 20 Nov. 1993, p. D7.

Watson, Scott, "Whose Nation?" *Canadian Art* (Spring 1993).

Weiss, Rachel, "Interrogating Identity," *High Performance* 56 (1991).

Young Man, Alfred, "The Savage Civilian and the work of Rebecca Belmore," in Daina Augaitis and Sylvie Gilbert, eds., *Between Views* (Banff, Alberta: Walter Phillips Gallery, 1991), pp. 37–39.

List of works

33 pieces

1. *Untitled,* 2001
sound installation with table, speakers, cardboard
boxes, chairs, audio equipment
variable dimensions

2. *Manifesto,* 2001
installation with shredded paper, wall-mounted
pencil sharpener, graphite marks, pencil shavings
variable dimensions

3. *Indian Land,* 2001
wall installation with 166 flags, electric fan
170 x 400 cm

4. *Rose,* 2001
Part 1: wall-mounted shelf with tea kettle, tea tray,
teapot, mugs, wicker basket, teabags, lemons,
sugar, napkins, knife and spoons
40 cm x 120 cm
Part 2: rose, photograph and wall-mounted shelf
with tea cup, saucer and burning candle
90 x 40 cm

5. *Untitled,* 2001
wall-mounted installation with glass eyes in plaster
3 x 11 cm

6. *Untitled (Oka, Ipperwash, Burnt Church,
Saskatoon, Nunavut),* 2001
wall-mounted installation with plaster, stencilled
letters and hair
123 x 45 cm

7. *Untitled,* 2001
paper shirt, pins, poem by Kateri Damm
98 x 72 cm

8. *Untitled,* 2001
wall-mounted work with sawed pieces of spruce
trunk, 4-inch construction nails
328 x 41 cm

9. *Black Cloud,* 2001
charred wood, nails, bed of salt
50 x 118 x 70 cm

10. *Untitled,* 2001
wall-mounted installation with plaster-dipped rags
231 x 210 cm

11. *Mister Luna,* 2001
wall-mounted installation with light bulbs and pair of
yellow shoes
80 cm (dia.)

Video Recordings

1. *Creation or Death, We Will Win,* 1991
performance with red rope and sand
Havana Biennial, Cuba (11 min., sound)

2. *High-Tech Teepee Trauma Mama,* 1987
performance of a song
Definitely Superior Gallery, Thunder Bay, Ontario
(3 min., sound)

3. *Bury my Heart,* 2000
performance with violinist, chair, carnations, blood
and water sprinkler
Paris Gibson Square Museum, Great Falls, Montana
(27 min., sound)

4. *The Indian Factory,* 2000
performance with numerous materials and props
assisted by performer Osvaldo Yero
AKA Gallery, Saskatoon, Saskatchewan
(60 min., sound)

Acknowledgements

The Blackwood Gallery's program owes much to the enthusiasm and generosity of the Director/Associate Dean of Humanities, Michael Lettieri, and to his assistant, Lucy Gaspini; also to the members of the Board of the Blackwood Gallery, including Evonne Levy, Jill Caskey, John Armstrong, Richard Sewell, Bogomila Welsh and Cyndra Macdowell; and to work-study students and gallery assistants Jessie Caryl, Gia Pereira, Carol-Ann Ryan and Iva Stoytcheva. The realization of this catalogue would not have been possible without the intelligence and commitment of Jessie Caryl, Curatorial Assistant (summer 2001) and the assistance of the *Young Canada Works in Heritage Institutions* through the Canadian Museums Association. The exhibition installation owes a great deal to the generous assistance of Osvaldo Yero and Michael Beynon. Much appreciated is the financial support from The Canada Council's Exhibitions and Publications Assistance program. I would also like to thank Sylvie Gilbert, Johanna Householder and Clive Robertson for their insightful contributions to the round-table discussion *Performance as Document* on February 13, 2001. My thanks are due to Dot Tuer for her passionate essay for this catalogue, and most of all to Rebecca Belmore for her perseverance, commitment and generous spirit, many thanks.
Barbara Fischer, Curator

Editing: Susan Harrison
Design: Andrew Di Rosa / SMALL
Printing: CJ Graphics, Toronto
Photography: Michael Beynon and courtesy of the artist; Paul Couillard
(p.23 top)

The Canada Council for the Arts
Le Conseil des Arts du Canada

National Library of Canada Cataloguing in Publication Data

Belmore, Rebecca
        Rebecca Belmore : 33 pieces

Includes bibliographical references.
Catalogue of an exhibition held at the Blackwood Gallery, Jan. 15 – Feb. 18, 2001.
ISBN 0-7727-8203-2

        1. Belmore, Rebecca—Exhibitions. I. Fischer, Barbara, 1956 –
II. Tuer, Dot III. Backwood Gallery. IV. Title.

N6549.B445A4 2001   709'.2   C2001-902481-9

wilderness poem # 1

eyes lowered body bent forwa
move slowly with care
through this wilderness that is
then when you leave there will
echoes of your sounds
a barely discernible path
and a few ashes from your fire
swirling in the wind
like a warning
then the wilderness will remain
untamed as it should be
and you will emerge
with clean hands
and the will to survive